DEAR PEN PAL

PLEASE WRITE
ME A LETTER

Raffi Songs to Read®

Like Me and You

Illustrated by Lillian Hoban
Words and music by Raffi and Debi Pike

YOUR FRIEND,

Crown Publishers, Inc., New York

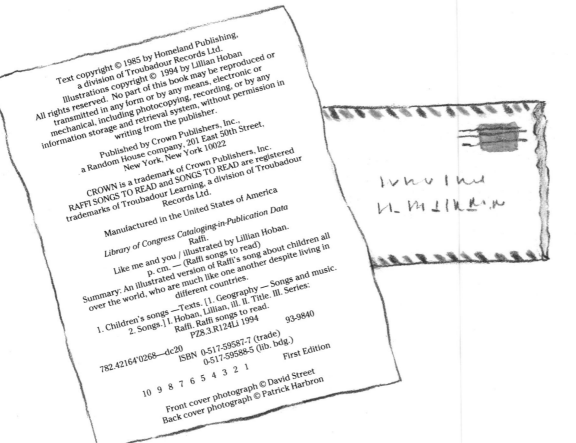

Published by Crown Publishers, Inc.,
a Random House company, 201 East 50th Street,
New York, New York 10022

CROWN is a trademark of Crown Publishers, Inc.
RAFFI SONGS TO READ and SONGS TO READ are registered
trademarks of Troubadour Learning, a division of Troubadour
Records Ltd.

Manufactured in the United States of America

Library of Congress Cataloging-in-Publication Data
Raffi.
Like me and you / illustrated by Lillian Hoban.
p. cm. — (Raffi songs to read)
Summary: An illustrated version of Raffi's song about children all
over the world, who are much like one another despite living in
different countries.
1. Children's songs —Texts. [1. Geography — Songs and music.
2. Songs.] I. Hoban, Lillian, ill. II. Title. III. Series:
Raffi. Raffi songs to read.
PZ8.3.R124Li 1994   93-9840
782.42164'0268—dc20   ISBN 0-517-59587-7 (trade)
                                    0-517-59588-5 (lib. bdg.)
10 9 8 7 6 5 4 3 2 1   First Edition

Front cover photograph © David Street
Back cover photograph © Patrick Harbron

Janet lives in England,

Pierre lives in France,

Bonnie lives in Canada.

Ahmed lives in Egypt,

Moshe lives in Israel,

Bruce lives in Australia.

Ching lives in China,

Olga lives in Russia,

Ingrid lives in Germany.

Gita lives in India,

Pablo lives in Spain,

José lives in Colombia.

And each one is much like another.

A child of a mother and a father.

A very special son or daughter.

A lot like me and you.

Koji lives in Japan,

Nina lives in Chile,

Farida lives in Pakistan.

Zosia lives in Poland,

Manual lives in Brazil,

Maria lives in Italy.

Kofi lives in Ghana,

Rahim lives in Iran,

Rosa lives in Paraguay.

Meja lives in Kenya,

Demetri lives in Greece,

Sue lives in America.

And each one is much like another.

A child of a mother and a father.

A very special son or daughter.

A lot like me and you.

Like Me and You

Words & music by Raffi, Debi Pike

Moderately, with feeling

1. Jan - et lives in Eng - land, Pierre lives in France, Bonnie lives in Can - a - da.

Ah-med lives in E - gypt, Mo - she lives in Is-ra-el, Bruce lives in Aus-tra-li-a.

Ching lives in Chi - na, Ol - ga lives in Rus - sia,

In-grid lives in Ger - man-y. Gi - ta lives in In - di - a, Pab-lo lives in Spain, Jo -

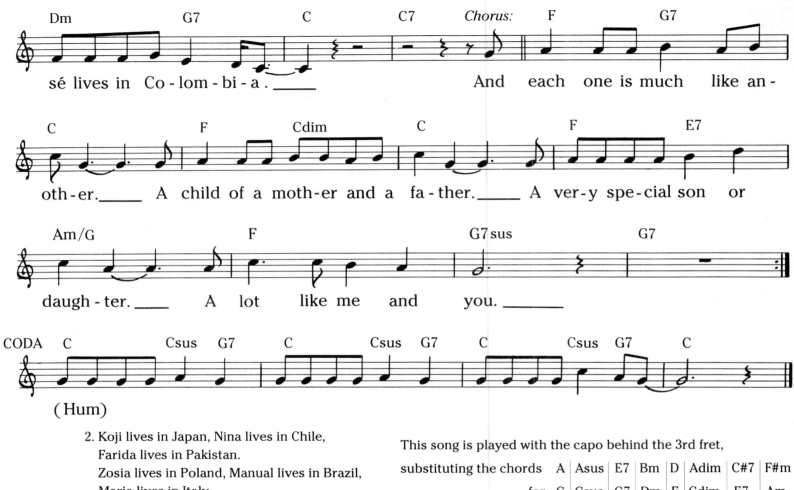

sé lives in Co-lom-bi-a. _____ And each one is much like an-oth-er. _____ A child of a moth-er and a fa-ther. _____ A ver-y spe-cial son or daugh-ter. _____ A lot like me and you. _____

(Hum)

2. Koji lives in Japan, Nina lives in Chile,
   Farida lives in Pakistan.
   Zosia lives in Poland, Manual lives in Brazil,
   Maria lives in Italy.
   Kofi lives in Ghana, Rahim lives in Iran,
   Rosa lives in Paraguay.
   Meja lives in Kenya, Demetri lives in Greece,
   Sue lives in America.

Repeat chorus

This song is played with the capo behind the 3rd fret,

substituting the chords	A	Asus	E7	Bm	D	Adim	C#7	F#m
for	C	Csus	G7	Dm	F	Cdim	E7	Am

Triangle